Improve your aural!

Paul Harris and John Lenehan

Contents

fabermusic.com

© 2006 by Faber Music Ltd
First published in 2006 by Faber Music Ltd
3 Queen Square London WC1N 3AU
Music processed by Music Set 2000
Design by Susan Clarke
Printed in England by Caligraving Ltd
All rights reserved

0-571-52458-3

CD recorded in Rectory Studio, High Wycombe, April 2006
Created and produced by John Lenehan
Thanks to Godstowe School Chamber Choir 2006
Track 26 ℗ and © 1988–2006, licensed by kind permission of Naxos Rights International Ltd
All other tracks
℗ 2006 Faber Music Ltd
© 2006 Faber Music Ltd

FABER **ff** MUSIC

Why is aural important?

You may wonder why you have to do aural at all. The answer is, that aural will really help you improve as a musician. And this may surprise you – it will help perhaps more than *any other* single musical skill.

Aural is all about understanding and processing music that you hear and see, in your head. By doing so, you will find that your own playing improves enormously. You will be able to play more expressively and stylistically, be more sensitive to quality and control of tone, your music reading will improve, you will be able to spot your own mistakes, be more sensitive to others when playing or singing in an ensemble, be more aware of intonation, improve your ability to memorise music and improve your ability to improvise and compose.

All the many elements of musical training are of course connected. So, when working through the activities in this book you will be connecting with many of them. You'll be listening, singing, clapping, playing your instrument, writing music down, improvising and composing – as well as developing that vital ability to do well at the aural tests in your grade exams!

Aural is not an occasional optional extra – just to be taken off a dusty shelf a few days (or even hours) before a music exam. It's something you can be developing and thinking about all the time. And as you go through the enjoyable and fun activities in these books you'll realise how important and useful having a good musical ear (being good at aural) really is.

How to use this book

When you have a few minutes to spare (perhaps at the beginning or end of a practice session), sit down with your instrument, by your CD player, and open this book. Choose a section and then work through the activities – you needn't do much each time. But whatever you do, do it carefully, repeating any activity if you feel it will help. In fact many of the activities will be fun to do again and again. And make sure that you come back to the book on a regular basis.

So, good luck and enjoy improving your aural skills!

Paul Harris and John Lenehan

For U.S. readers:
Bar = Measure
Note = Tone
Tone = Whole Step

Clapping rhythms

As part of Test C for Grade 4, you will have to clap or tap back a rhythm. Hearing, understanding and memorising rhythms is an important and useful skill. It will help you in learning new pieces, playing or singing in an ensemble and in your sight-reading.

17/09.
ncat
10m ✓

listening activities

1 On each of these four tracks you'll hear a short phrase played three times. After each one is played twice, clap it back. You'll hear it a third time – then stop the CD and write the rhythm down.

track
2

$\frac{2}{4}$

track
3

$\frac{2}{4}$

track
4

$\frac{3}{4}$

track
5

$\frac{3}{4}$

tracks
6-15

2 Here are ten more short phrases. Clap each one back after you've heard it played twice.

track
16

3 You will be asked whether the music is in 2, 3 or 4-time. Sometimes the difference between 2 and 4 is difficult to detect. In 2-time you are likely to hear more strong pulses than in 4-time. Music in 4-time is more inclined to have longer phrase lengths and fewer accents. On this track there are some examples of music by Beethoven in either 2 or 4-time. Write down the time of each example.

1 _____   2 _____   3 _____   4 _____   5 _____   6 _____

track
17

4 This track contains examples in either 2, 3 or 4-time. After you've heard each one, write down what time it is in.

1 _____   2 _____   3 _____   4 _____   5 _____   6 _____

5 Here are some phrases to clap or tap back. Write down whether they are in 2, 3 or 4-time. Each one is played twice.

1 ____   2 ____   3 ____

4 ____   5 ____   6 ____

6 After you've heard each phrase in this waltz, improvise your own answer. The first one is done for you as an example. Use elements from the given phrase in your responses.

7 Using a piece you are currently learning, clap or tap the rhythm of the whole piece with your right hand (on a table, for example) and the pulse with your left hand. Now repeat, swapping hands. Now tap the pulse with your right foot and clap or tap the rhythm.

8 Now try to hear the first four bars of the piece in your head, and then, without looking at the music, have a go at answering the following questions:

● How many beats are there in each bar? _____

● Does the piece have an up-beat? _____

● Is it in simple or compound time? _____

● Are there any rests in the first four bars? _____

● If so, what are they? _____

● Write down the rhythm of the melody of the first four bars. Put in the clef and the time signature:

Come back and repeat this exercise using other pieces or using other four-bar phrases from the same piece.

Section 2 Pitch

On your instrument, play the first six notes of any major scale.
Choose a scale that is comfortably in your singing register.

Now sing the notes as numbers, to the following rhythm:

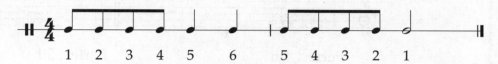

1   2   3   4   5   6   5   4   3   2   1

listening activities

track 25 **1** An interval is the distance between two notes. Listen to each of the two-note intervals on this track. You'll hear the interval and then a well-known tune that uses that interval either at, or very near the beginning. Connect the intervals to the tune.

Doh ray

| major 2nd | | While shepherds watched their flocks by night |

Doh mez

| major 3rd | | Twinkle, twinkle, little star |

Doh fah

| perfect 4th | | The holly and the ivy |

Doh soh

| perfect 5th | | Good King Wenceslas |

Doh la

| major 6th | | Away in a manger |

Solfa and hand signals

5

2 Now play the following. Listen carefully as you play each interval.

Major 2nd   Major 3rd

Perfect 4th   Perfect 5th

Major 6th

3 Now hear each of these intervals in your head and then sing them:

1st – 2nd note (Major 2nd)

1st – 3rd note (Major 3rd)

1st – 4th note (Perfect 4th)

1st – 5th note (Perfect 5th)

1st – 6th note (Major 6th)

4 Now hear the following tunes in your head (the notes are represented by numbers). Pauses and accents have been put in to help you with the rhythm. Do you recognise them? (The composers are Johann Strauss, Dvořák and Grieg)

```
          >        >
1.   1  1  3  5  5
```

```
      ⌢      ⌢         ⌢                    ⌢
2.   3  5  5  3  2  1  2  3  5  3  2
```

```
3.   5  3  2  1  2  3  5  3  2  1  2  3  2  3  5  3  5  6  2  6  5  3  2  1
```

Each piece will be revealed on this track.

5 On this track you'll hear six tunes. Write down the interval between the first two notes. It will be either a Major 2nd, Major 3rd, Perfect 4th, Perfect 5th or Major 6th. Be careful about the last interval – it's one you've met before, but it is not listed here.

1 _____ 2 _____ 3 _____

4 _____ 5 _____ 6 _____

6 Listen to this track and write down which number (or 'degree') of the scale the tune ends on. The first one is done for you.

1 ___2___ 2 _____ 3 _____

4 _____ 5 _____ 6 _____

7 On this track there are some phrases for you to sing back. Sing your responses as soon as you've heard the piano play the phrase twice.

8 This track contains more examples of tunes to sing back. Sing them back after you've heard them played twice.

Singing from notation

In Grade 4 you will have to sing, from notation, a sequence of notes that go both above and below the key-note.

Choose a low note in your singing range and sing (using numbers) one octave of a major scale ascending and then back down to the fifth:

1 – 2 – 3 – 4 – 5 – 6 – 7 – 8 – 7 – 6 – 5

Now sing the final four notes again:

8 – 7 – 6 – 5

In all of the following examples, play each exercise on your instrument after you've sung it to see whether you were accurate. (Don't forget to adjust the notes if you play a transposing instrument.)

1 8 – 7 – 6 – 8
2 8 – 7 – 6 – 5
3 8 – 6 – 7 – 5
4 8 – 6 – 5 – 8
5 8 – 5 – 6 – 7 – 8

Now write the notes of the above examples out in G major. The first one is done for you:

Now hear each one in your head and then sing it from notation.

Here are some more examples to sing: *Sing in various keys.*

Now write down the three previous exercises in the key of F major. The first is done for you.

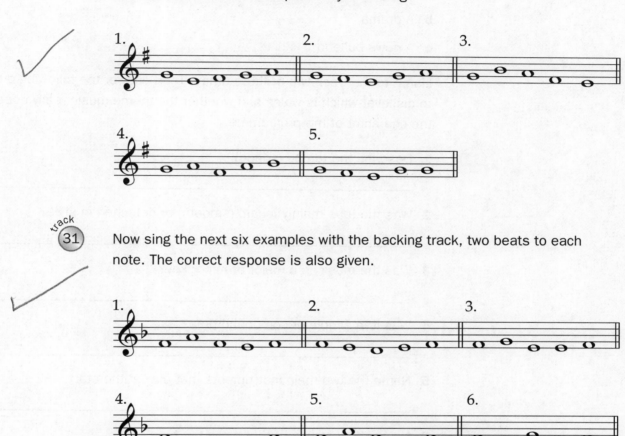

Then hear them in your head and finally, sing them from the notation.

Here are some more examples for you to sing:

Now sing the next six examples with the backing track, two beats to each note. The correct response is also given.

Do ray me fah soh la ti Doh

Learning to listen to music

In addition to the areas already introduced, in Grade 4 you will be asked to talk about the *character* or *mood* of a short piece of music.

On the next tracks you'll hear three TV-like themes:

a A comedy

b A drama

c A news bulletin

Listen to the track two or three times. Then answer the following questions to discover which is which and whether the theme music really does reflect the character of the programme.

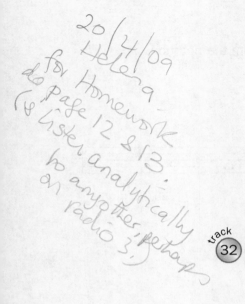

track
32

1 Describe the tempo (speed).

_____

2 Was the tune mainly *legato* (smooth) or detached in style?

_____

3 Was the music in a major or minor key?

_____

4 Was it in simple or compound time?

_____

5 Name the two main instruments that play at the start.

_____

6 Name the instrument that plays the tune.

_____

7 How would you describe the character?

_____

8 Was it a comedy, drama or news bulletin?

_____

track 33

1 Describe the tempo (speed).

_____

2 Was the music mainly *legato* (smooth) or detached in style?

_____

3 Was the music in a major or minor key?

_____

4 Was it in simple or compound time?

_____

5 Was the accompaniment smooth or detached?

_____

6 Were there any changes in the dynamic levels?

_____

7 How would you describe the character?

_____

8 Was it a comedy, drama or news bulletin?

_____

track 34

1 Describe the tempo (speed).

_____

2 What instrument plays the fast scale at the beginning?

_____

3 Was the music in a major or minor key?

_____

4 Was it in simple or compound time?

_____

5 What happened to the dynamic level at the end of the piece?

_____

6 How would you describe the character?

_____

7 Was it a comedy, drama or news bulletin?

_____

listening activities

1 On these tracks you'll hear six short pieces. From the words below, choose one that best describes the character of each piece. There may be more than one suitable answer.

War-like	Jaunty	Perky	Angry
Gloomy	Spooky	Flowing	Serene
Lilting	Jagged	Elegant	Explosive

track (35) _____   track (36) _____   track (37) _____

track (38) _____   track (39) _____   track (40) _____

2 The next five tracks comprise short pieces that combine all the features you might be asked about. Each piece will be played only once and then you will be asked two of the following questions:

1 Where was the quietest part of the music?

2 Was the music in a major or a minor key? Did it change anywhere?

3 How would you describe the character?

4 Did the tempo change anywhere?

5 Which section was smooth?

6 Were the dynamic changes sudden or gradual?

track (41) _____   _____

track (42) _____   _____

track (43) _____   _____

track (44) _____   _____

track (45) _____   _____

3   Listen to track 45 again and make up a story to fit the music.

_____

_____

_____

_____

_____

_____

_____

_____

4   Using a piece you are currently working on, answer the following:

- How would you best describe the character of the music? Why?

_____

- Is the piece in a major or minor key?

_____

- Do the dynamic markings help to bring character to the music?

_____

- Play the piece really exaggerating all the markings!

- Play the piece reversing all the markings (e.g. $\textbf{\textit{p}} = \textbf{\textit{f}}$, cresc. = dim., rall. = accel. etc.)

- Play the piece as expressively as possible, making the most of all the markings.

Section 5 # Making connections

These fun activities show you how aural connects with all the other aspects of music. Choose one or two each time you practise.

... with memory

Think about a piece that you've recently learnt and then try to 'replay' the whole piece in your head from memory. Now try playing as much as you can from memory on your instrument.

... with tone quality

Choose a four-bar phrase from a piece you are currently learning and play it from memory, concentrating on producing your best tone quality.

... with perceiving errors

On this track the musicians are less than perfect in their performances. One player can't keep the pulse steady (out of time), another has learnt some wrong notes (wrong notes), one can't keep together with his fellow players (bad ensemble), and another can't play in tune (out of tune). Using the words in brackets, write down which is which.

1 _____   2 _____

3 _____   4 _____

... with improvisation

On this track you'll find a piece in a dreamy style. After each two-bar phrase, improvise your own dreamy response to the flute playing. The key is F major – just use the notes: F G A C D (For B♭ instruments, improvise in G major using the notes: G A B D E. E♭ instruments improvise in D major, using the notes: D E F♯ A B)

... with sight-reading

Choose a sight-reading piece* and try to hear it first in your head. Then play it.

... with intervals

Play a note and then, in your head, hear the note a perfect 4th above (e.g. play C and then hear F). Sing the note and then play it to see how accurate you were. Can you find any perfect 4ths in the pieces you are currently studying?

*From *Improve your sight-reading!* Grade 4, for example

... with scale patterns

Listen to this track and then connect the correct boxes:

major scale	played 1st
melodic minor scale	played 2nd
harmonic minor scale	played 3rd
chromatic scale	played 4th

... with musical style

On this track, you'll hear four examples of dances in $\frac{3}{4}$ (minuets or waltzes). Using the information given, connect the correct boxes.

Baroque music
The two, independent melodic lines sometimes imitate each other. You'll hear some ornamentation too.

played 1st

Classical music
Classical dances are elegant, simple and in clear four-bar phrases.

played 2nd

Romantic music
Romantic dances are often flamboyant and very expressive.

played 3rd

20th/21st-century music
Dances written in the 20th or 21st centuries will often move in unexpected directions.

played 4th

A final message from the authors!

Answers

(by CD track number)

Section 1: *Clapping rhythms*

16 1: 2   2: 4   3: 4   4: 2   5: 2   6: 4

17 1: 3   2: 4   3: 3   4: 2   5: 2   6: 4

18–23 1: 2   2: 4   3: 3   4: 2   5: 2   6: 4

Section 2: *Pitch*

25 Major 2nd – Good King Wenceslas, major 3rd – While shepherds watched their flocks by night, perfect 4th – Away in a manger, perfect 5th – Twinkle, twinkle, little star, major 6th – The holly and the ivy

27 1: Major 3rd   2: Perfect 4th   3: Major 2nd   4: Major 6th
5: Perfect 5th   6: Minor 3rd

28 1: 2   2: 3   3: 1   4: 5   5: 6   6: 4

Section 4: *Learning to listen to music*

32 1: Moderate   2: *Legato*   3: Minor   4: Simple
5: Bass guitar and piano   6: Horn   7: Serious   8: Drama

33 1: Fast   2: Detached   3: Major   4: Simple   5: Detached   6: No
7: Jaunty   8: Comedy

34 1: Fast   2: Trumpet   3: Major   4: Compound   5: *Diminuendo*
6: Urgent   7: News bulletin

35 Flowing or serene

36 War-like or angry

37 Jagged or jaunty

38 Spooky

39 Elegant or lilting

40 Jaunty or perky

41 Minor (changes to major in the middle)/Sudden

42 Jaunty, playful/Yes, at the end (speeds up)

43 At the end/March-like

44 No/Gradual *crescendo* to the end

45 Minor: Major at the end/The final section

Section 5: *Making connections*

46 1: Out of time   2: Wrong notes   3: Out of tune   4: Bad ensemble

48 Harmonic minor scale, major scale, melodic minor scale, chromatic scale

49 Romantic, Baroque, 20th/21st Century, Classical